Introducing Oil Painting

Introducing Oil Painting

Michael Pope

B. T. Batsford Limited, London
Van Nostrand Reinhold Company, New York

I dedicate this book to my Bank Manager who stopped
me procrastinating

© Michael Pope 1969
First Published 1969
Reprinted 1971
Library of Congress Catalog Card Number 76–81152
7134 2409 5

Printed and bound in Denmark by
F. E. Bording Limited, Copenhagen
for the Publishers
B. T. Batsford Limited,
4 Fitzhardinge Street, Portman Square, London, W.1
and
Van Nostrand Reinhold Company,
430 Park Avenue, New York, N.Y. 10022

Contents

Foreword

The aim of this book is to help the student of painting to produce technically sound paintings at the minimum cost to himself. Wherever possible I have suggested the cheapest source of supply for any materials needed to make up the recipes or formulae.

Naturally a good artists colourman can supply the artist with all the prepared materials he needs, but, as I have stressed throughout the book, one pays dearly for this service. Whereas if you prepare your own canvases and painting media you do so at a fraction of the cost and usually better, because you prepare exactly what you require. Wherever possible the recipes in the book are expressed in 'Parts By Measure'. Very few artists have scales and measuring jugs in their studios and the P.B.M. method is accurate enough for nearly all the recipes given.

Supports

Textiles
Selecting a textile

Most painters prefer to paint on a textile as a support because of its textural quality and pleasant 'give' to the brush.

The most suitable types of textiles for the painter are those which have the following qualities:

1 Are closely woven, with a stout slightly uneven threat without knots.
2 Are woven with the threads at right angles to one another thereby ensuring even stretch.
3 Only stretch slightly.
4 Are either white or an even colour throughout.

A good linen generally has these four qualities. Some linen is specially made for painters and is obtainable in three grades: fine, medium and coarse.

Linen crash is rather fine but has many knots.

Linen scrim is strong but widely woven.

Hessian is very coarse and needs a good deal of priming if it is used. Cotton should not be used because it is too thin and lacks elasticity.

The cheapest way to buy canvas is to buy a whole roll either from the mill or from a scenic artists' suppliers or even a ship's chandler and sail manufacturer.

Opposite
Detail of *Doña Isabel Corbos de Porcel* by Goya
Oil on canvas
Very thin paint throughout the painting which is underpainted in greys and then thinly glazed on top. The blouse is a very broad white impasto which has been glazed pink. The thin black paint of the mantilla becomes a transparent glaze in places and the pink sleeves of the blouse show through. Probably painted with a wax oil medium

Reproduced by courtesy of the Trustees, The National Gallery, London

9

10

The larger the quantity you order the cheaper it is and it is worth while for two or three painters to club together and then to split up the roll between them. Canvas can be obtained 'ready primed', and reputable artists' colourmen produce good well-primed canvas in a variety of grades. But you only have to work out the difference in cost to realise how much more economical it is to prepare your own canvas.

Stretchers

Stretcher pieces should be made of good quality seasoned wood and should butt together tightly when joined, to form right-angled corners. Very large stretchers usually have one or more cross-pieces to prevent the stretched canvas from warping.

All artists suppliers make stretcher pieces which they sell in a large range of sizes.

Stretching a canvas for oil painting

1 Assemble the stretcher pieces, checking that the bevelled edges are all facing the same way, then knock together with a mallet or a piece of wood.
2 Make sure that the stretcher is square by measuring across the diagonals with a piece of string.
3 Cut a piece of canvas 2 in. larger all round than the stretcher and place the assembled stretcher on this, with the bevelled edges face down.
4 Tack one side in the middle of the outer edge.
5 Pull canvas taut and knock a tack in the opposite side.
6 Repeat with the other two sides.
7 Return to the first side and knock in two tacks, each 2 in. either side of the centre one, straining the canvas as you do so.
8 Continue to do this in the same sequence until the canvas is tacked to within 2 in. or 3 in. of each corner.

Opposite
1 *Top row left to right*
Four linen flax canvases with varying degrees of tooth
Bottom row left to right
1 Linen crash (note the faults which occur frequently)
2/3 Cotton canvases with close and open weaves
4 Bleached linen canvas

9 Finish the corners by pulling and folding the canvas as in figures 7, 8, 9 and 10.

10 Insert the wedges but do not hammer into place. When stretching primed canvas it is advisable to use a pair of canvas pliers (6) to pull the canvas taut. If you keep the tension even throughout, no creasing will occur. The canvas can be stapled to the stretcher in the same way as described for tacking; it makes a much neater edge and enables the canvas to be removed more easily if required, at any time.

2   Tools required

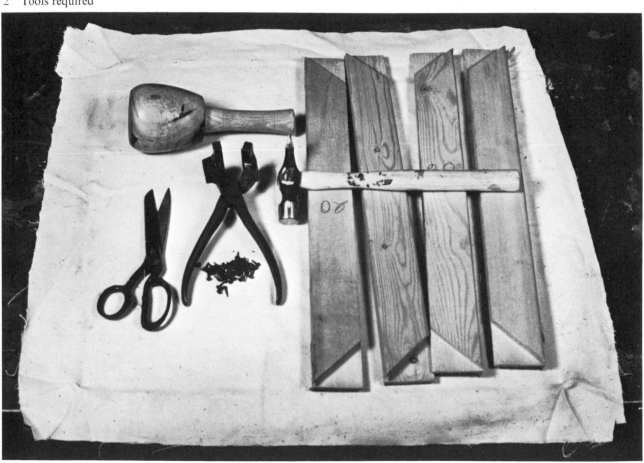

3 Knocking stretcher together

4 Squaring up the stretcher
5 Squared stretcher laid on cut canvas

6 Pulling canvas tight with canvas pliers
7 Pulling canvas tight by hand

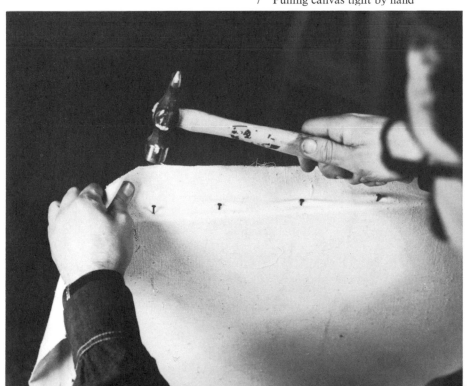

8   Folding the corner

9   Folding the corner

12 The stretched canvas
11 Tacking the corner

10 Folding the corner

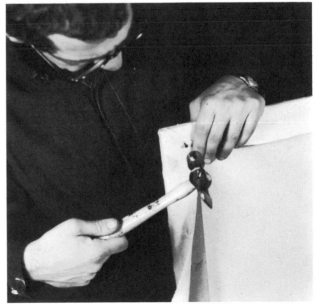

Mounting textile on board

A good cheap support can be made by sticking thin textile on to board. A textile such as butter muslin can be stuck on to a compressed board, hardboard, masonite or essex board with glue size and then primed with any of the accepted primers.

Cut the butter muslin large enough to fold over on all sides. Then size both sides of the board with strong glue size. Whilst wet lay the butter muslin on the board and brush the size into the textile to make a firm bond. Turn the excess muslin over the back and stick with more size. Lay flat until dry. The support can be primed with a standard ground or, better still, one especially economical for muslin mounted on board.

Recipe

Glue size	1 part by measure
Whiting	$1\frac{1}{2}$ parts by measure
Raw linseed oil	$\frac{1}{4}$ part by measure

Stir the whiting into the hot size and then add the oil slowly, stirring all the time.

Application

Rub one coat into the muslin with the fingers, whilst still wet brush on a second coat. Allow to dry for a week before using. If it is too absorbent, coat with 1:15 glue size.

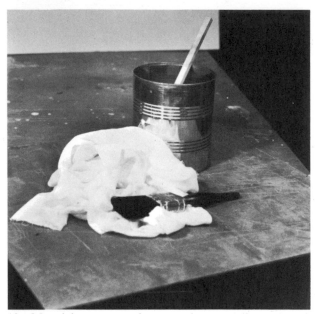

13 Materials necessary for mounting a textile on board. 7:1 glue size mixture, butter muslin, board, varnish brush

14 Sizing the board with 7:1 glue size mixture

15 Applying butter muslin to the board
17 Board covered with butter muslin

16 Finishing off round the back

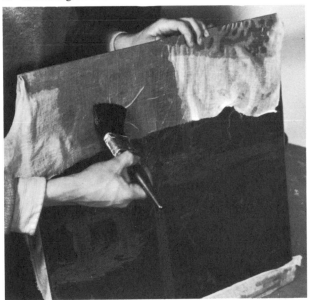

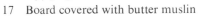

Wood

Wood can be a very durable support but it does tend to warp and crack, and to minimise these tendencies the wood must be selected with care. Oak or mahogany at least 1 in. thick and fully seasoned should be used. An old door or table is probably the best source of supply. 20 in. × 24 in. is the maximum size you should use, and even then it should be cradled to prevent warping.

The wood should be sized and primed on both the front and back.

Plywood

A good thick plywood 5:8 ply, preferably mahogany faced, makes a good support if sized twice on both sides. Mahogany has a better textural surface. Cradling will help to stop any warping.

Paper, Compressed boards and cardboard

Paper

A good rough-surfaced water-colour paper made from linen rag, makes an excellent support for oil painting. It needs only to be mounted on a piece of inert board such as hardboard with casein glue (*Casco*), and given one coat of casein size to counteract the absorbency. Glue size can be used.

Compressed board (hardboard, masonite, chip board)

Hardboard is an excellent support. The rough side has an unpleasant mechanical texture but the smooth side can be painted on without sizing or priming. All you need to do is to rub it down with some methylated spirits on a rag, to render it slightly more absorbent.

Chipboard is much coarser than hardboard and needs sizing before use. It is much heavier than hardboard and has a tendency to crumble at the corners.

Cardboard

Thick cardboard makes a fairly good support if sized on both sides. Lautrec and Sickert both used it frequently. Essex board is a plycard, very strong and useful as a support for mounting a textile.

Prepared painting boards

There are a number of prepared painting boards on the market, but they tend to have an unpleasant mechanical texture, besides being very expensive.

Conclusions

A stretched canvas is the most pleasant surface to paint on. Hardboard is the most durable. Perhaps a compromise of a textile mounted on a board is the best solution. Try out all the various painting supports and you will discover the one which suits you best.

18 Materials and equipment necessary for making size
19 Sprinkling powdered size on to cold water

Underpriming

An underpriming is used to isolate the fibres of canvas from the oil in the ground or the painting and also to counteract extreme absorbency in the support.

Size

Size is the most commonly used underpriming and is the name given to all weak solutions of glues made from animal matter.

The four main categories are those made from:
1   Leather waste, in sheet form.
    Rabbit skin glue, cologne glue, parchment glue.
2   Bone and cartilage, in granules.
    Commercial glue size, decorators' size.
3   Milk, in powdered form.
    Casein, *Casco*.
4   Fish—in liquid form.
    Isinglass, seccotine, *Croid*.

A good size should possess the two properties of 'adhesion' and 'gelation' in a balanced proportion.

Leather waste
Is the purest and best, but it is expensive.
Recipe
1½ oz sheet glue
1 quart cold water

Method
Break the sheet of glue into small pieces and allow it to soak in the cold water for 12 hours. Then heat in a double boiler until all the glue has dissolved—apply hot.

Commercial glue size
Contains many impurities but a good brand name will make a size solution quite suitable for most jobs and nearly all painters use it.

Recipe

Commercial glue size   1 P.B.M.
Water   7 P.B.M.

Method
Put a little cold water in a suitable can and sprinkle on the powdered size, stirring all the time. As the granules of glue swell, add more cold water until a smooth paste forms. Then either make up with very hot water or add the remainder of the water cold and heat gently until all the size is dissolved, stirring all the time. DO NOT BOIL—boiling denatures size and destroys all its adhesive and gelatinous qualities. It should be brushed on hot and when cold should set into a loose jelly, which will keep for two or three days.

Casein size
Pure casein will not dissolve in water without the addition of an alkali such as ammonium carbonate. But proprietary brands such as *Casco*—are so prepared that they will dissolve in cold water.

Recipe

Casein size   1 P.B.M.
Cold water   7 P.B.M.

Method
Sprinkle the size powder on to a little of the cold water and stir until dissolved then make up with the remainder of the cold water. Apply cold and use the same day.

Fish glue
Is not much used by painters as it lacks gelatinous qualities and is very brittle when dry.

20   Making up solution with hot water

Priming or ground

The 'ground' is the name given to the final surface applied to a support before the picture is painted on it. It is applied to give a good painting surface and stop excess absorbency which might exist with only an underpriming.

Types of grounds
Oil ground

An oil ground, because of its supple nature, is the best for stretched textiles. Most consist of white lead paste with enough thinner to enable them to be easily brushed. Zinc white, silica and whiting can all be added if desired. It has the advantage of being easy to make, coupled with the disadvantage of taking a long time to dry: 4 to 6 weeks.

Recipe

White lead paste	7 P.B.M.
Thinner	$3\frac{1}{2}$ P.B.M.

Thinner

White spirit	6 P.B.M.
Raw linseed oil	1 P.B.M.

Decorators' white lead paste is the cheapest way of making this ground. If you use a tube of lead white, such as Flake White, it will contain more oil than decorators' paste and can be thinned with spirit alone.

Opposite

Detail of *Snowstorm—Steamer off a harbour's mouth* by Turner
Oil on canvas

Turner used a very restricted palette on this painting. It was laid in as a series of vigorous white impasto strokes over a grey ground or underpainting and the definition of the imagery is brought about by the use of very thick glazes of ochres and blues. The looseness of the brushwork is exactly right for the stormy atmosphere which he was trying to capture

Reproduced by courtesy of the Trustees, The Tate Gallery, London

This ground should not be overthinned and it should be left for a month before painting on it. If by then, it is still too absorbent, give it one coat of shellac varnish.

Gesso or chalk ground

Because of its brittleness, a gesso ground is only suitable for a rigid support such as wood or hardboard but it can be applied so as to produce an exceptionally smooth white surface.

Receipe I

1:7 glue size mixture	1 P.B.M.
Whiting	1 P.B.M.

Method

Sieve the dry pigment into a little of the hot size until a thick smooth paste is made and then add the remainder of the size mixture. Keep warm in a double boiler whilst making and applying.

Recipe II

5:1 casein size	1 P.B.M.
Whiting	10 P.B.M.

Method

Add a little of the cold water to the powdered casein size, leave for 15/20 minutes then add the rest of the cold water. Sieve the whiting into the mixture and stir. In both these recipes, powdered zinc white can be added to the whiting to increase the whiteness of the ground.

Emulsion ground

An emulsion is a physical combination of a watery substance with that of a non-watery substance.

Example: Milk, egg yolk.

It is an example of the colloidal state.

Recipe

Half chalk ground.

1:7 glue size mixture	1 P.B.M.
Whiting	1 P.B.M.
Zinc oxide	1 P.B.M.
Raw linseed oil	$\frac{1}{3}/\frac{1}{2}$ P.B.M.

Opposite
Dans le parc de Chateau Noir by Cézanne
Oil on canvas
Thinly painted throughout in a very close range of blues and blue greens. The trees in the foreground are delineated to accentuate their form and position in space. This also helps to counteract the strong diagonal movement of the rocks. The warm areas of colour are exclusively in the bottom half of the painting, with the strongest patches around the focal point of the picture. This sparing use of complementary colours gives the painting a quality of enormous richness and greatly heightens the visual impact. (See page 75)

Reproduced by courtesy of the Trustees, The National Gallery, London

21 Materials necessary for economical gesso ground. 7:1 glue size mixture chalk and zinc white

22 Sieving the dry materials into the size mixture

23 Force the powdered chalk and zinc white through sieve with your fingers

24 Applying the hot ground

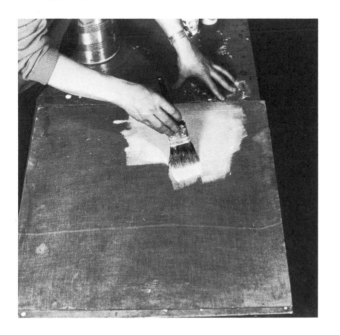

25 Applying the ground with the brush loosely in every
direction

Method

1 Always use glue size, not casein, as casein tends to yellow the oil.
2 Mix together all the dry pigments and break up any large lumps.
3 Add enough hot size to make into a stiff paste.
4 Add the linseed oil drop by drop, beating in well.
5 Add the remainder of the hot size stirring all the time.
6 If the mixture is too thick add more size.
7 Keep hot in a double boiler.
8 Apply with a brush.

Properties

1 Mid-way between an oil and a chalk or gesso ground.
2 Less brittle and less absorbent than a chalk ground.
3 Dries quickly and can be used within a week.
4 Easy to apply.
5 Can be applied to boards or stretched canvas.

Commercially prepared grounds

All the artists' colourmen market at least one oil primer and they do not differ very much in either price or quality.

A good quality lead-based undercoat paint, which can be bought from a builders' merchant or paint store, makes a good economical priming. But check that it does not contain too great a quantity of artificial drier and that it is oil based and not an artificial resinous paint.

Acrylic ground

Acrylic grounds are sold for use with acrylic-based colours, but they can be used as priming for oil painting and they should be applied directly to the canvas or board without previous underpriming with size. The basis of all the acrylic paints is a plastic resin like polyvinyl acetate, and this can be purchased more cheaply by the gallon from decorators' merchants.

It can be used 'straight' in which case it will dry as a completely transparent film or one can stir in whiting or zinc white powder to produce a white priming. To extend it use only water and make sure that the surface to which you apply it is free from all oil and grease before you lay it on.

Tools and equipment

Palettes

There is a wide range of palettes available in a variety of shapes, sizes and materials. The classic palette (26) (made of mahogany) is cut to fit the arm, and balanced. Rectangular palettes are popular, but nowadays all shapes and sizes of palettes are obtainable either in wood or plastic.

It is simple to make a palette out of plywood, formica or hardboard.

If you buy a new wooden palette, or make one, it is advisable to rub it daily with linseed oil for a week in order to fill the fibres and stop the wood absorbing the oil from the colours.

If you have a permanent studio then you can use what is the best of all palettes, a slab of marble on your painting table.

26   Classic shaped palette

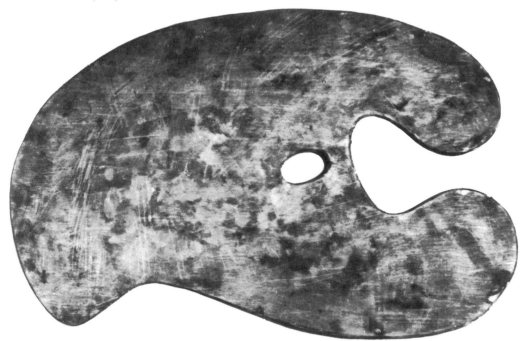

27 Rectangular sketching palette with two types of dipper

28 An easy way to clean a neglected palette. Pour a little
   paraffin on the palette

29 Set fire to palette for 30 seconds

31 Author's palette. A slab of marble from a Victorian washstand

Dippers

Dippers are designed to clip on to a palette and hold oil and turpentine. The double dippers are the most useful and should be large enough to hold plenty of oil and turpentine without overfilling.

Brushes

Oil-painting brushes are made either from sable, or more commonly, hog hair. The bulk of your brushes will be of hog hair, and the type and size depends on personal preference.
The main shapes are: Flat, Round, Filbert.

Brushes should always be cleaned after use by first flushing out all surplus paint with turpentine and then washing with soap and warm water. This will not damage the brush if it is a good one, and the only brushes worth buying are the best, cheap brushes lose their shape and wear out very quickly.

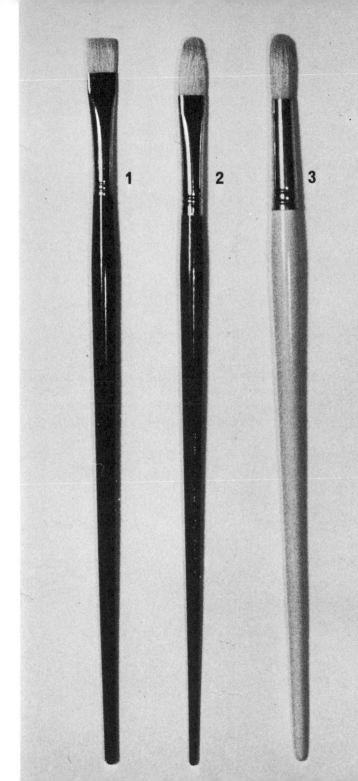

32 Three types of hog's-hair brushes
1 flat, 2 filbert, 3 round

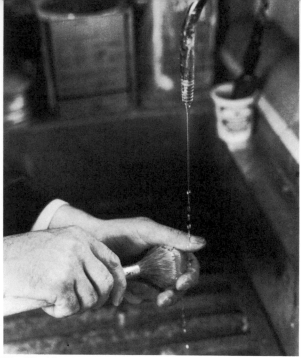

33 Washing brush with soap and warm water
34 Working lather into the brush by revolving in the palm of the hand

35 Smoothing brush back into shape by stroking in the palm of the hand

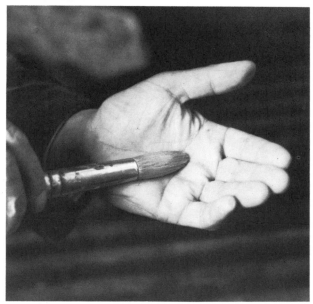

Extending the life of worn brushes

Even when brushes are very worn their life can be extended by heating the ferrule with a match and pulling out the hair a fraction with a pair of pliers.

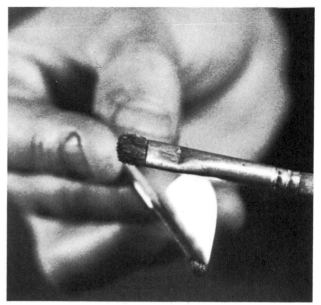

36 Heat the ferrule of the brush with a match
37 Pull out the bristles a fraction with a pair of pliers

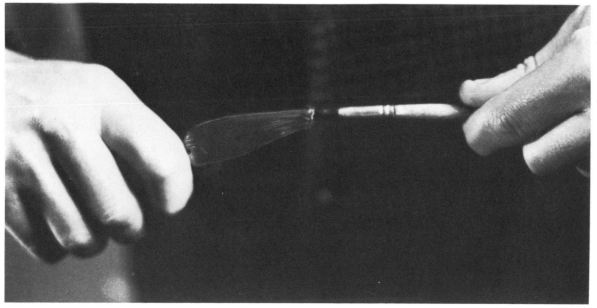

38 Squash the end of the ferrule with a pair of pliers
39 Trim the bristles with a pair of scissors

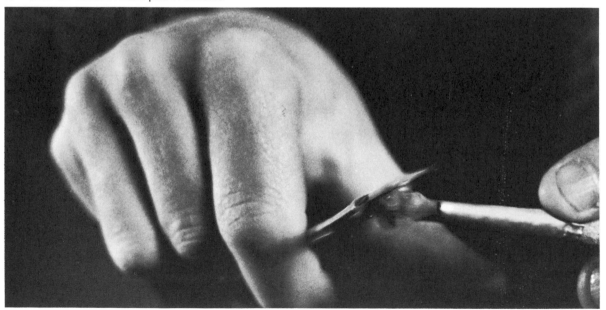

Knives

Palette knives: a palette knife, as its name implies is used for mixing colours on the palette and also for scraping the palette clean after use. If you have a painting table with a marble slab as a palette, a decorators' stripping knife is the best instrument for cleaning the slab.

Painting knives: these knives are invaluable for laying an impasto and most painters have a couple. There are dozens of shapes to choose from, but in choosing one you should look for a flexible blade and preferably one which has been formed from the shank itself and not welded on. The best knives come from France.

40   Various palette knives and painting knives

Easels

The old 'studio easel' has almost been replaced by the 'radial easel', which is a pity because if you have a permanent studio, there is no doubt that they are the sturdiest and most easily adjustable of them all. You can still pick them up occasionally in junk shops and some manufacturers still make small studio easels.

The 'radial easel' is a good strong easel with probably a greater range of adjustment than any others and it can be folded into a compact bundle for storage.

There are many sketching easels on the market, some of them so complicated in design that merely assembling them is a creative act in itself.

If you need a sketching easel, buy the simplest one which is capable of taking a fair-sized canvas and is adjustable to three positions.

41   Radial easel

Brush cleaning can

Take a fair-sized can and fold a piece of perforated zinc so that it makes a platform about 1 in. from the bottom of the can. Then just cover this with white spirit.

The surplus paint which you wash out of your brushes will fall through the holes and stay as a sludge beneath the zinc, leaving the white spirit clean.

42 Fitting zinc mesh base into paint cleaning can

43 Cleaning paint off brushes in paint cleaning can

Colours

Pigments

The coloured pigments used in the manufacture of all paints are the same whether the paint be oil, water-colour, gouache, tempera or acrylic. The medium used to bind the pigment determines which kind of paint it will be. Of course, some pigments are more suitable ground in one medium than another; lead white for example is almost exclusively an oil-paint pigment.

Pigments for oil colours are generally ground in one of the drying oils, linseed, poppy or walnut. The oils most commonly used are poppy and linseed, walnut oil being rarely used these days.

Chemical properties of pigments

The perfect permanent pigment would be one which was chemically and physically inert and stable. That is to say there would be no reaction between it and other pigments, it would be unaffected by either acids or alkalis and it would not change its character when subjected to heat, light or moisture. By these criteria, viridian, cobalt and carbon black are probably the most permanent.

Physical properties of pigments

The usefulness of a pigment in painting depends to a large extent on its physical properties, its colour, the body or tinting power, opacity or transparency, how it absorbs and reacts with oil and the shape and size of the pigment grains.

The pigments can be divided into two main groups:

1 Organic compounds—those made from animal or vegetable matter.

   Animal: Indian yellow, sepia, carmine, bone black.

   Vegetable: Madder, vine black, indigo, gamboge.

2 Inorganic compounds—these are made from various chemical compounds.

   Oxides: Zinc white, earth colours.

   Sulphides: Cadmiums.

   Carbonates: White lead.

   Chromates: Chrome yellow, chrome green.

Manufacture

Pigments are either mined in a natural state, or manufactured artificially. Although some pigments are obtained by a combination of both processes. The earth colours which are, in their natural state, clays stained with compounds of iron or manganese are amongst the most permanent of the pigments.

Yellow Ochre	Light Red
Raw Sienna	Indian Red
Raw Umber	Venetian Red
Terre Verte	Burnt Sienna
Vandyke Brown	Burnt Umber

All these colours are either found in their natural state, prepared by roasting or by heating with iron compounds. Nowadays by-products of industry provide an alternative source of supply for most of them. Pigments are manufactured artificially either by heating chemical compounds, to produce such colours as artificial vermillion, zinc white, artificial ultramarine, cobalt and cerulean blue; or by precipitation from solutions of such colours as chrome yellow, cadmium yellow, lemon yellow and prussian blue.

The Whites

White lead

Basic carbonate of lead: $2\,PbCO_3 - Pb(OH)_2$

White lead is probably the most versatile of all the white pigments used by the painter. It has stood the test of time and although some manufacturers claim that titanium white is better and safer to use, lead white is still the most widely used.

Properties

(a) It is poisonous and should always be bought ground in oil
(b) It is susceptible to sulphurous fumes
(c) To its credit it is extremely opaque
(d) Quick drying in oil
(e) Has good brushing qualities
(f) Very durable.

Flake White

A proprietary name given to basic carbonate of lead with the addition of a small percentage of zinc oxide. The makers claim that the zinc oxide improves the working consistency and helps maintain whiteness.

Silver White

Flake White.

Cremnitz White

Pure basic carbonate of lead.

Foundation White

A proprietary name for white lead ground in linseed oil instead of poppy oil, which is the binder generally used.

White lead paste

This is white lead ground in a minimum of linseed oil and one buys it by the pound weight from builders and decorators' merchants. It is slightly silvery in colour due to impurities but it is much cheaper and many painters (including myself) prefer its consistency to that of the artists' Lead White sold in tubes. The best way to keep it and stop it forming a skin is to put it in a glass jar and cover it with water.

Zinc White

Zinc oxide—ZnO

Zinc white is prepared by burning metallic zinc in an oxidising atmosphere. It was first introduced as an artist's pigment in 1834.

Properties

(a) Non-poisonous and slightly antiseptic
(b) Less opaque than white lead
(c) Very slow drying due to the interaction of zinc with the oil
(d) Dries slowly
(e) Produces a soft, slightly crumbly paint film
(f) Fairly high oil absorbency.

Permanent White

Permanent White is the trade name for a white oil paint which consists of titanium white with the addition of a small percentage of zinc white ground in poppy oil.

One of the unfortunate things about oil painting is that more often than not, the best colours are the least permanent and most likely to change when mixed or subjected to strong light.

Some artists worry themselves sick about what is going to happen to their painting in the future and others slap paint on with an abandon only equalled by their technical ignorance. My inclination lies somewhere between these two extremes. I think that posterity is quite capable of looking after itself but that the painter has a certain obligation to his client and should be prepared to guarantee that his painting is not going to fade or fall off the canvas for at least 20 years. A minimum of craftsmanship will ensure this.

Most artists colourmen now list their prepared oil colours in three or four grades of permanence from 'absolutely' permanent to 'fugitive', and all can substitute a similar permanent colour for most of the fugitive colours.

Factors affecting permanence of pigments

Atmosphere
Sulphurous fumes in the atmosphere tend to affect certain pigments, especially the metallic-based pigments such as lead white.

Medium
The yellowing of oil will affect some pigments, and change their colour, chrome yellow tends to green with age. Certain driers in prepared mediums may react with some pigments. Litharge, PBO is one of these but I consider that the flexibility of the medium more than compensates for the slight discolouration of certain pigments.

Light
Strong sunlight can cause photo-chemical reactions with some colours and this will result in either a dimming of the intensity or a darkening, depending on the colour affected. Aniline dyes, madder, sepia and carmine are all likely to react to the action of sunlight.

Interaction of pigments

Some pigments interact with each other when mixed. The sulphides will chemically react with metallic pigments and cause the metallic pigments to blacken. Sulphurous compounds such as artificial ultra-marine, vermillion and the cadmiums should not be mixed with iron-based compounds like prussian blue: copper-based such as emerald green, or lead-based, Flake White and chrome yellow.

Fugitive pigments

The following pigments are not at all stable and should be avoided if possible:

Emerald green

(Paris green) $(Cu(C_2H_3O_2)_2, 3Cu(AoO_2)_2)$.
This colour should not be mixed with any other colours, especially sulphurous compounds.

Chrome yellow

Lead chromate. $PbCrO_4$.
This colour is susceptible to sulphurous compounds and also tends to turn green when ground in oil.

Mauve

A synthetic dye. Amino-phenylamino ptolyldito-lazonum sulphate. $C_{27}H_{25}N_4 (SO_4)\frac{1}{2}$. Tends to fade and discolour.

Earth colours

Ochres

Yellow Ochre
Transparent Golden Ochre
Red Ochre
Brown Ochre
Indian Red
Light Red
Tuscan Red
Venetian Red
A natural earth containing hydrated iron oxide $Fe_2O_3H_2O$ in the case of the Yellow Ochres.

The Red Ochres contain a mixture of anhydrous ferric-oxide Fe_2O_3 and the anhydrous oxide and the colour varies depending on the percentage and quality of ferric-oxide in the clay.

All the Ochres are permanent and stable colours.

Siennas

Raw Sienna is a yellow ochre named after its place of origin, Sienna. It has a warmer tint than yellow ochre

Opposite
Detail of *Water Lilies* by Monet
Oil on canvas
The underpainting is a very thick blue/green wash with the subsequent colours laid more thickly with a scumbling technique. The brush marks are used to define the images and throughout the picture the underpainting shows through, unifying the more positive passages. The paint film is matt which probably means that Monet used his paint very dry with a little medium possibly beeswax and turpentine. When viewed from a distance of 12 ft the effect is one of shimmering light. The lilies read against the background without any delineation merely because of the heightened colour and the more vigorous brushwork
Reproduced by courtesy of the Trustees, The National Gallery, London

and is more transparent. Burnt Sienna is made by calcining Raw Sienna.

Both are very permanent and used extensively in glazing.

Umbers

Raw Umber. A pigment belonging to the same family as the Siennas and Ochres but in addition to ferric-oxide it contains manganese dioxide.

Burnt Umber. This is made by roasting Raw Umber and the resultant colour is much warmer and transparent.

Terre Verte (green earth).

Paint manipulation

Essential oils

Essential oils are volatile oils obtained from plants and trees. Unlike the fatty oils they evaporate and a good rectified oil should evaporate completely. A way of testing an essential oil is to put a drop on to a piece of blotting paper and then check the amount of resinous residue left after evaporation, a good oil will leave little or no residue.

Turpentine
Turpentine is made by distilling the resinous sap of pine trees. A good turpentine will evaporate leaving only a trace of rosin.

Oil of spike (lavender oil)
This oil evaporates more slowly than turpentine and has a very pleasant smell, but otherwise its characteristics are not unlike turpentine. It is very much more expensive than turpentine.

Venice turpentine
A sticky oleo-resinous liquid obtained from the european larch (*douix decidua*) with a strong pinaceous smell. It is useful as a medium when mixed with stand oil.

Strasbourg turpentine

Obtained from the silver fir with similar properties to Venice turpentine. It is expensive and not much used these days.

Mineral spirit

Mineral spirit is a distillation of crude petroleum oil. It is used by many artists as a thinner to replace pure turpentine and by nearly all as a brush cleaner. It is cheap if bought by the gallon from decorators' merchants.

Natural drying oils

These oils are usually used as binders or vehicles for pigments. As binders their job is:
1   To bind together the pigment particles.
2   To ensure adhesion of the pigment to the painting surface.
3   To protect the pigment from varying atmospheric conditions.
4   To dry quickly as a transparent and elastic film which will not discolour with age.

The most widely used oils are linseed oil and poppy oil.

Linseed oil

Linseed oil is the most widely used of all the vegetable drying oils and is obtained from the seeds of flax. It can be bleached by exposure to the sun or by chemical means, but it invariably returns to its natural light yellow colour in time and it would seem better to accept this condition and buy good quality natural oil from an artists' colourman or chemist.

It drys by a process of oxidation, into a transparent leathery film. In the beginning this drying process is rapid but it slows down as surface film is formed, and complete drying can take years. If one paints over partially dry paint the old paint surface acts like a sponge and absorbs the oil from the new paint, causing it to sink. This can be counteracted by painting thinly in the beginning with lean paint, i.e. little oil and gradually adding oil in the successive coats of paint.

Poppy oil

Poppy oil is obtained from the seeds of the opium poppy. It has similar properties to linseed oil but is slightly paler in colour and tends to be slower in drying. Artists' colourmen prefer to grind most of their colours in poppy oil because of these properties.

Stand oil

If linseed oil is heated in an absence of air for several hours a molecular change takes place and the resultant oil is darker and thicker than raw linseed oil. Stand oil dries quicker than raw linseed and as well as producing a more durable paint film it discolours less. The old method of producing stand oil was literally to stand it in the sun in loosely-covered glass jars for a number of weeks until it thickened. The change was effected by partial oxidisation and polymerisation of the oil which became bleached by the sun.

Artificial drying oils

Artificial drying oils are basically natural drying oils with soluble chemicals added which act as catylists and hasten the process of oxidisation.

The three most commonly used additives are:

Compounds of cobalt

Cobalt naptathenate, cobalt linoleate thinned with turpentine to a 6% solution. One drop of a weak solution added to a spoonful of the painting medium will suffice to hasten the drying.

Manganese oxide

A strong drying oil can be made by adding manganese oxide to linseed oil.

| Manganese oxide | 1 P.B.M. |
| Linseed oil | 3 P.B.M. |

Lead acetate

This dryer is very violent in action and is not really considered safe to use.

Painters have always used artificial driers, some with unfortunate results but if they are used sparingly they are a great aid to paint manipulation as long as one remembers that excessive use will:

1 Destroy the binding power of the oil.
2 Cause cracking.
3 Discolour certain pigments.
4 Unless used throughout the whole painting, cause unequal drying which will lead to stress lines in the paint film.

Cobalt driers are probably the best of the ones in use.

Varnishes

Varnishes are either made by dissolving a resin in an essential oil such as turpentine or oil of spike, or in a fatty oil like linseed. The first group are called soft resin varnishes and the second hard resin varnishes.

Copal varnish

Copal varnish is the best known of the hard resin varnishes. It is less used now than it was previously because of the difficulty of removing it from paintings in need of restoration. It can be made in the studio, but it is difficult and it is better to buy it from an artists' colourman.

Mastic varnish

Mastic varnish is made from resin dissolved in either turpentine or alcohol. It is not a good varnish because it yellows and blooms.

Dammar varnish

Again is resin dissolved in turpentine or alcohol. It does not bloom or yellow like Mastic and is easy to make in the studio.

Recipe:
Dammar resin (crushed) 1 P.B.M.
Pure turpentine   4 P.B.M.
Crush the resin and tie it in a piece of butter muslin,
suspend this bag in a container containing the turpentine
for 24 hours or until all the resin has dissolved. Bottle
the varnish and cap tightly.

Shellac varnish

Shellac varnish can be bought from artists' colourmen
or decorators' merchants but it is very easy to make in
the studio. It is mainly used for coating a ground which
is too absorbent, i.e. a gesso or an emulsion ground
but it also serves as an economical fixative for charcoal
drawings.
Recipe:
Shellac   1 P.B.M.
Alcohol   6/7 P.B.M.
Drop the shellac into a bottle of alcohol and shake it
frequently until it is all dissolved.

Painting media

Painting media are used to make the oil paint more
tractable and to ensure that the layers of paint are
balanced. A painting medium is a vehicle or binder
which holds the particles of pigment together, and not
merely a diluent such as turpentine or petroleum
spirit. Artists who grind their own colours generally
grind them into a workable state with the medium so
that there is no further need to add more.

Most artists these days use tube oil paints, which are
colours already ground in either linseed or poppy oil,
and to these they add a medium of their choice either
to extend the colour or to accelerate the drying. The
most commonly used medium is a mixture of linseed
oil and turpentine to the proportions of 60% oil to
40% turpentine, any of the drying oils can be substi-
tuted for linseed and the artist generally enriches his
mixture by adding more oil as the painting progresses,

following the old adage of always painting 'fat over lean'. The disadvantage of using an oil and turpentine mixture is its long drying time and the difficulty of manipulating the paint if it is greatly thinned in order to glaze.

A varnish medium
Recipe 1:

Dammar varnish	9 P.B.M.
Genuine turpentine	9 P.B.M.
Stand oil	4 P.B.M.
Venice turpentine	2 P.B.M.

Use this as a medium in which to grind dry pigments or as a medium for the dilution of tube colours.

Recipe 2:

Copal varnish	1 P.B.M.
Linseed oil	1 P.B.M.
Genuine turpentine	1 P.B.M.

A varnish stand oil medium
Recipe:

Venice turpentine	3 P.B.M.
Stand oil	1 P.B.M.

Beeswax medium
Recipe

Beeswax	1 P.B.M.
Genuine turpentine	3 P.B.M.

Break the beeswax into small pieces. Warm the turpentine in a double boiler and then stir in the beeswax until it all dissolves.

Allow to cool and put into a wide-necked container. This medium is particularly good for oil painting on a gesso ground. One of its qualities is that the paint film tends to dry slowly with a semi-mat finish.

Ruben's medium
Recipe

Raw linseed oil	10 P.B.M.
Litharge (PbO)	$\frac{1}{16}$ P.B.M.
Beeswax	2 P.B.M.

Opposite
Detail of a painting showing an area of white impasto which has been laid in with a painting knife and subsequently glazed with ochre and alizarin, also applied with a painting knife. A wax/oil medium. Ruben's medium was used. The use of a wax/oil medium makes it possible to lay areas of transparent colours with a knife

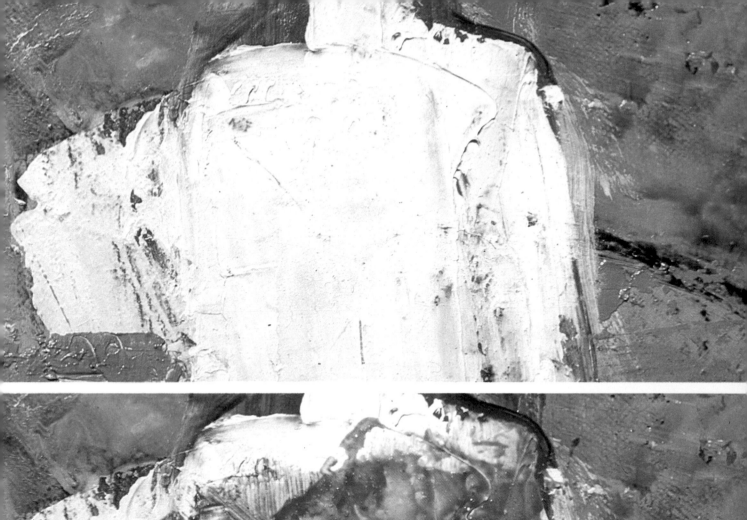

Grind the litharge carefully in a little oil, it is poisonous. Heat the remainder of the oil slowly in a large-necked vessel (a tin washing up bowl is ideal) then add the litharge and beeswax, heat to 250°C, stirring frequently. When the liquid turns black and heavy brown fumes rise, it is cooked. It is advisable to make this medium out of doors on an open fire because the smell of it cooking is revolting and the fumes are toxic. When it has cooled a little you may pour it into pots and it will then set into a 'black butter'.

This medium tends to discolour all colours slightly but its versatility more than compensates for this disadvantage. It is equally good for laying thick impastos and thin glazes, it dries quickly because of the litharge and it keeps the paint film flexible for years. I have canvases painted with this medium which have been tightly rolled and stored for 10 years and there is not the trace of a crack in the paint film.

Maroger's medium
Maroger's medium is a commercial product sold under this name and it is an emulsion of boiled linseed oil, mastic varnish, gum arabic and water. It is quite nice to work with.

Synthetic resin mediums
All the colour manufacturers now have a 'house medium' prepared from synthetic resins. They tend to be thixotropic in character and are good in every respect except price.

Opposite
Detail of a painting in which the underpainting has been underlaid with thin impasto using a knife and then glazed with ochres and blues. Wax/oil medium. Ruben's medium was used

45 Put linseed oil in can first and heat before adding beeswax and litharge

44 Materials and equipment necessary for making Ruben's medium. Linseed oil litharge (Pbo) and beeswax. Stove and large-necked can

46 Stirring the mixture whilst cooking

The painting

Staining a canvas

Until the introduction of manufactured primed canvases, artists prepared their own canvases with the priming of their choice which they usually coloured by introducing into the ground a neutral coloured pigment such as terre verte or red ochre.

Artists' colourmen sell their prepared canvases primed with a white ground and it is left to the painter to decide whether he paints directly on to a white ground or stains his canvas first. I prefer to start painting on a neutral ground which enables one to work easily from light to dark without that awful moment when you make the first mark on a virgin white canvas and immediately condition all subsequent brush marks.

If you make any of the grounds suggested in this book you can introduce pigment into the ground itself in order to tone it, or you can stain the white ground afterwards with oil paint.

As a general rule a mixture of ultramarine and black, or yellow ochre and black make the best neutral stains.

47 Materials necessary for staining a canvas. Genuine turpentine, yellow ochre or ultramarine and black

48 Cover the canvas as shown with alternate dabs of ochre
and black
49 Pour turpentine on to the surface

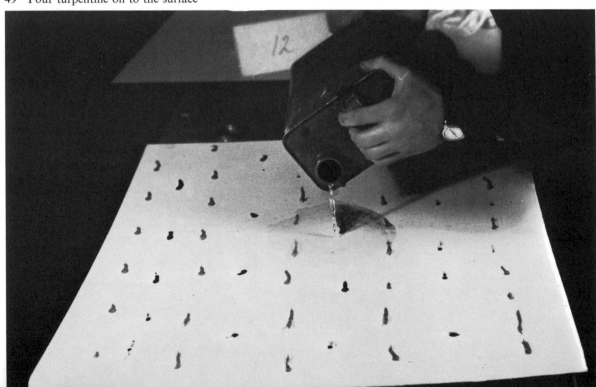

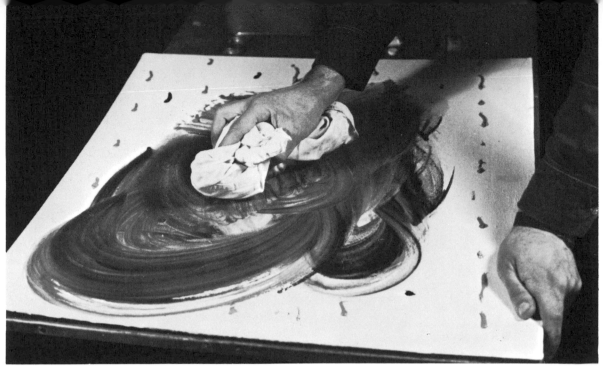

50   Wipe the canvas with a rag until the paint is mixed and evenly distributed

51   Wipe the canvas with parallel strokes until an even tone is achieved

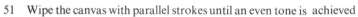

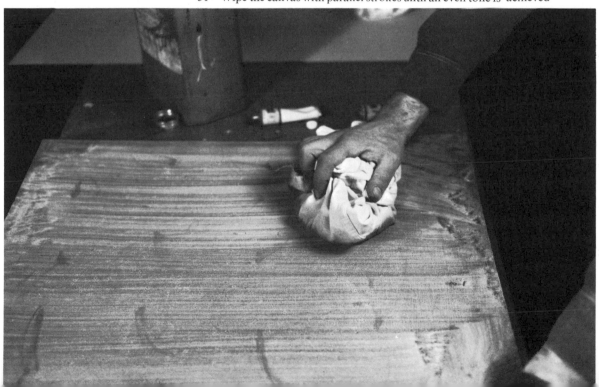

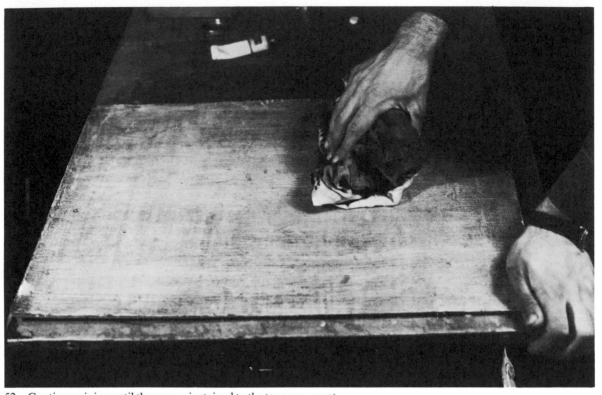

52   Continue wiping until the canvas is stained to the tone you want

Transferring the design

There are many ways of transferring a drawing to the canvas. The easiest way is to define the limits of the drawing to the same scale as the prepared canvas and then to square up the drawing and the canvas to a suitable scale, i.e. 1 in. : 2 in., 1 in. : 4 in.

If the drawing is particularly intricate each individual square can be sub-divided again as many times as required. The original drawing need not be damaged in this process because one can lay a piece of tracing paper over it and square up on this.

If one is working on a composition from a series of separate drawings, it is sometimes a good idea to draw the finished composition on a piece of tracing or thin paper to the same size as the canvas. This enables one to trace the drawing straight on to the canvas by first rubbing the back of it with charcoal or powdered graphite and using a pencil or a sharpened stick to trace off the design.

53   Chalk drawing before squaring up

54 Squared-up drawing

55 Drawing and canvas squared up to a scale of one to two

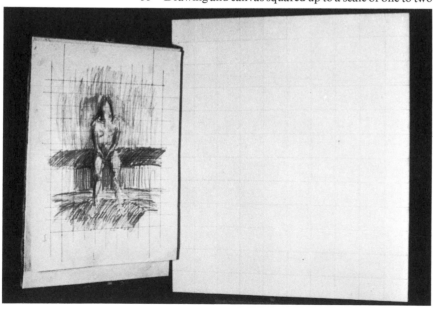

56 Preliminary drawing in thin paint on the canvas

Underpainting

Having laid in the basic design on the canvas it is then time to establish something of the colour and tonal range of the painting. It is advisable to use as few colours as possible, well diluted with a diluent such as turpentine plus a little oil or medium so that they are merely stains on the canvas. One tends to lay in these first stains with a large hogs-hair brush and in doing so the charcoal or pencil drawing is sometimes washed away and this means redrawing with a neutral colour using a smaller hogs-hair or sable brush. Alternatively, a thin spray of charcoal fixative can be applied before beginning painting.

Having once covered the canvas and established a basic tonal relationship throughout the painting it is then much easier to mix body colours which will work together tonaly in an ordered way.

Some painters paint their whole painting in a range of neutral greys, only adding colour at the end by glazing. This method certainly produces a painting of extremely rich colour but it is really only possible by the use of a medium such as one of the new thixotropic media or that based on Ruben's medium. I personally think that this medium is the most versatile of all the painting mediums and if it is used throughout a painting there is no need to varnish the painting afterwards, because the oil and wax in the medium prevent all colours from sinking. One disadvantage is that by using this medium it is impossible to paint a picture with a 'mat' finish.

57 First thin washes laid in order to establish basic tonal relationships

58 Second stage—the paint is still a thin stain

59   Third stage—underpainting completed

60   Developing the painting by laying in opaque body colours

61 Scraping off paint with painting knife in order to correct a mistake

62 Wiping remaining paint off with a rag soaked in turpentine

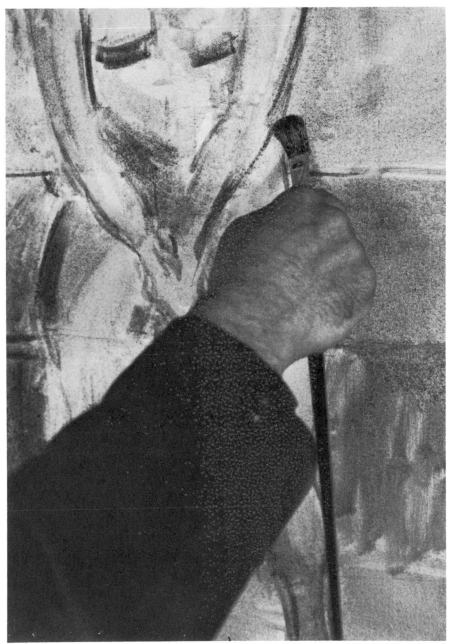

63 Correct way to hold a brush

64 Making mahl stick. Folding rags over the end of a 3 ft. cane

65 Forming rags into a ball

67 Mahl stick in use

66 Tying rags tightly to the cane

The painting itself

Range of colours

If you examine paintings by painters noted as colourists you find that it is the way certain colours are used together and not an enormous range of colours that give these paintings their quality.

A landscape by Cézanne might look fantastically rich and colourful, but if you examine it you realise that the painting is basically a blue painting and that 95 per cent of the colour ranges from blue through blue/green to green and that these colours are rendered more brilliant by the addition of small areas of complementary or near-complementary colours. In fact I think it is true to say that most paintings are basically monochromatic.

Layout of the palette

Every painter has his own ideas about what range of colours he should have on his palette. Mine is strongly biased towards blues. There is no perfect palette, it depends so much on 'what' and 'how' you paint. Probably the best advice is that everyone should experiment as much as possible and then restrict his palette to the minimum.

My idea of a comprehensive palette is:

Flake or Titanium White
Cadmium Yellow (pale and deep)
Golden Ochre (transparent)
Cadmium Red (deep)
Ultramarine
Cerulean Blue
Cobalt Blue
Viridian
Cobalt Green
Black

In actual fact I have a far greater range of colours in my studio, but more often than not a painting is completed and only four or five colours have been used throughout.

Once again, 'how' you place your colours on the palette is very much a matter of personal preference. I tend to put my colours wherever I have room on my palette, depending on how recently I have cleaned it. But one of the generally accepted methods is to place the colours around the edge of one's palette starting with white and running through the yellow, reds, blues, greens, earth colours and finishing with black. Some painters lay out their colours in the order of the spectrum, everyone will have their own personal preference. Personally I do not think it makes a scrap of difference as long as it suits your method of working and you lay out an ample supply of each colour. If you do not use all the colour it can always be scraped off the palette at the end of the day and put under water where it will keep fresh until needed again.

68   Mixing paint on the palette with a knife

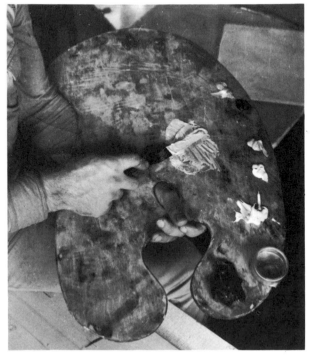

69 Scraping surplus paint on to a piece of glass

70 Storing surplus paint in a jar of water

71 Paint thinned greatly with turpentine showing cracking
72 Materials and equipment for grinding paint. Marble slab and glass muller, linseed oil, wax medium and pigment

Paint quality

Consistency of paint

If you grind your own colours the paint should be ground in the medium you intend to use and will therefore be of the right consistency. But if you use tube colours you will find that they all vary in their consistency, some are dry and others, like black, very oily. The best way of unifying them and solving this problem is to use a good medium which will help to stabilise the drying time of all the colours.

Thin paint

If paint is merely thinned with turpentine or petroleum spirit it will dry very quickly but the paint film will crack within a very short time. If you wish to prove it, take a little black, thin it greatly with spirit and paint a piece of canvas with it. It will dry mat and crack within hours. Paint should only be thinned in this way in order to stain canvases which are going to be overpainted with properly balanced paint.

As a general rule all paint should be thinned with a properly balanced medium.

Textures

It is not considered technically sound to add substances such as sand to one's paint in order to give a textured surface to the paint film. But many painters do this and it is again a question of media. Oil paint sand and turpentine will soon fall off the canvas but a good medium will probably bind the sand to the surface as it does the colour pigment.

The new acrylic resins are quite capable of binding substances like sand to the painting surface.

The textural quality of most painting is produced by the way in which the artist used his brush or painting-knife, and this is a very personal thing which only comes by practising one's craft.

Impasto

An impasto is only a heavy application of paint made either by brush or painting knife. Some painters paint in such a way that one could say that the whole surface is one of impasto but generally an impasto is laid to emphasise or heighten a particular part of a canvas and more often than not, this paint is laid in whites or greys as a basis for subsequent glazing.

Glazes

A glaze is a transparent film of paint laid over an under-painting. The quality of a glaze is created by the light passing through the transparent film of colour and being reflected back by the paint beneath. This means that the paint beneath must be light in colour in order to reflect the light, so that one generally finds that a glaze is best laid over a white or light neutral grey.

If light is to pass through a film of paint it is obvious that the paint must be greatly thinned with a medium. Linseed oil is no use for glazing as it does not stay where you put it, a medium which is thixotropic in character is necessary, preferably one which contains beeswax such as 'Ruben's Medium'.

Painting with a knife

Painting with a knife usually implies a very heavy, slab-like paint texture but this is not the only way of applying paint with a knife. By laying heavy paint and then scraping off the excess, one can manipulate the paint on the canvas with a circular motion of the painting knife until one has a very thin paint film. This process can be repeated again and again, allowing some of the underpainting to show through, until a very rich surface texture is obtained without the paint film being tremendously thick.

73 Adding oil to the pigment on the marble slab

74 Working the pigment into the oil with a spatula

75 Correct way to hold the muller

76 Grinding the colour with a circular motion

77 Scraping the paint back into the centre of the marble slab

78 Scraping the muller

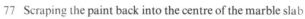

Polymer paints

The last few years have seen a great increase in the use of polyvinyl compounds as binding media for artists' pigments. The success of synthetic resins used in the manufacture of commercial paints encouraged artists' colour manufacturers to produce a paint ground in a synthetic resin. The most commonly used resin is polyvinyl acetate and this is used in a colloidal state dispersed in water, it is milky white in colour but dries into a completely transparent rubbery film. The manufacturers claim that this vehicle will not crack and is as durable as any oil paint binder. Time will tell.

One can buy the vehicle, polyvinyl acetate by the gallon from artists' colourmen or decorators' stores and as one only has to grind pigments in a little water before adding them to the P.V.A. it is very easy and very much cheaper to make one's own paint.

Advantages
1 Polymer paint can be applied to any painting surface, such as canvas or wood, without previously priming it.
2 Additives such as sand can be mixed with the P.V.A. to give textural surfaces.
3 Paint can be diluted with water and used thinly without fear of cracking.
4 The paint dries very rapidly.

79 Working with P.V.A. medium on a flat canvas

Disadvantages

1 Paint will not adhere to greasy surfaces. One cannot paint over oil paint, but one can paint in oils over a P.V.A. ground.
2 Dries so fast that one has to continually wash out ones brushes in water to prevent them caking hard.
3 The paint does not have the body which oil paint has and it is just a little like painting with toothpaste.
4 A normal palette cannot be used because of the cleaning difficulty, the best palette for use with P.V.A. colours is a sheet of glass which can be scraped clean with a razor blade.

The colour manufacturers sell a special priming for use with polymer colours but I have found that a coat of raw P.V.A. diluted with a little water is sufficient to seal canvas or wooden supports.

80 Textural effect made by mixing sand with P.V.A.

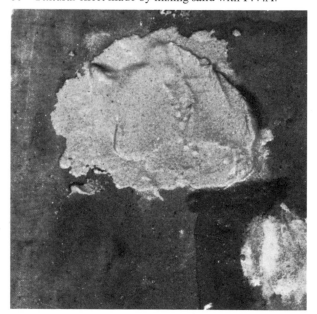

Glossary

Backing   Protection to prevent atmospheric damage to canvas, panels, paper and board, etc.

Beeswax   Wax secreted by bees, varies in colour from white to yellow.

Binder   The medium or vehicle which holds the pigment particles together in the paint.

Body colour   Colours made with pigments with a good covering power.

Boiled oil   Linseed oil heated with lead, manganese of cobalt oxides to facilitate drying.

Cradling   Method of reinforcing the back of wooden panels to prevent warping.

Diluent   Thin liquid used to dilute oils.

Dryer   Metallic salts added to drying oils in order to increase the rate of oxidation.

Emulsion   A physical mixture of two liquids in which drops of one liquid are suspended in the other. The condition is usually obtained by the introduction of a third substance as an emulsifying agent.

Fixative   A binding agent sprayed on to pastels to make them permanent.

Flat colour   An area of colour uniform in brilliance, tonality and value.

Glaze   A thin layer of transparent paint, usually painted over another colour.

Ground   A prepared surface on which colours are laid.

Impasto   A thick or heavy application of paint.

Mastic   A resin used in making varnish.

Opaque   Colour which is non-transparent.

Palette   Any flat piece of wood, metal, plastic or marble used by the painter as a surface on which to mix his paints.

Pigment   The powdered substance used as colouring matter in paint.

Support   The flat surface on which a painting is made, either canvas, wood, hardboard, metal or paper.

Wash   A thin coat of well diluted paint.

Bibliography

Painting Materials, A Short Encyclopedia, Rutherford J. Gettens & George L. Stout, Dover Publications Inc., New York

The Materials of the Artist and their Use in Painting, Max Doerner, Harrap, London in association with Harcourt Brace, New York

The Painter's Pocket Book of Methods and Materials, Hilaire Hiler, Faber, London

The Artist's Methods and Materials, Maria Bazzi, John Murray, London

The Painter's Craft, Ralph Mayer, Van Nostrand, New York

The Technique of Oil Painting, Colin Hayes, Batsford, London and Reinhold, New York

Formulas for Artists, Robert Massey, Batsford, London and Watson-Guptill, New York

Suppliers of artists' equipment and materials

Great Britain

General

Firms who either manufacture or supply almost everything the painter requires:

Lechertier Barbe Ltd, 95 Jermyn Street, London, S.W.1

L. Cornelissen and Sons, 22 Great Queen Street, London, W.C.2

Clifford Milburn Ltd, 54 Fleet Street, London, E.C.4

Reeves and Sons Ltd, Lincoln Road, Enfield, Middlesex

Robertsons and Co Ltd, 71 Parkway, London, N.W.1

George Rowney and Co Ltd, 10/11 Percy Street, London, W.1

Winsor and Newton Ltd, 51/52 Rathbone Place, London, W.1

Specialist

Firms who carry certain items mentioned in this book which are not usually held by the general artists colourmen, or, who are able to supply goods in bulk at a cheaper rate:

Bird and Davis Ltd, 52 Rochester Place, London, N.W.1
Manufacturers of artists' stretchers

Boots Chemist Ltd
Linseed oil, turpentine, litharge

A. Leete and Co, Ltd, 129 London Road, London, S.E.1
Powdered pigments, linseed oil, lead white paste, whiting

Brodie and Middleton Ltd, 79 Long Acre, London, W.C.2
Theatrical artists' colourmen, pigments, canvas

Russel and Chapple, 23 Monmouth Street, London, W.1
Raw canvas

U.S.A.

Grumbacher, 460 West 34th Street, New York, NY

The Morilla Company Inc, 43–01 21sr Street, Long Island City, New York and 2866 West 7th Street, Los Angeles, California

New Masters Art Division: California Products Corporation, 169 Waverley Street, Cambridge, Massachusetts

Permanent Pigments, Cincinnati, Ohio

Shiva, Paducah, Kentucky

Stafford-Reeves Inc, 626 Greenwich Street, New York, NY 10014

Weber and Co, New York, NY

Winsor and Newton Inc, 555 Winsor Drive, Secaucus, New Jersey 07094

Index